UNCOLLECT

Snow's on the fellside, look! How deep,
our wood's staggering under its weight.
The burns will be tonguetied
while frost lasts.

But we'll thaw out. Logs, logs for the hearth!
And don't spare my good whisky. No water, please.
Forget the weather. Elm and ash
will stop signalling
when this gale drops.

Why reckon? Why forecast? Pocket
whatever today brings
and don't turn up your nose, it's childish,
at making love and dancing.
When you've my bare scalp, if you must, be glum.

Keep your date in the park while the light's whispering.
Hunt her out, well wrapped up, hiding and giggling,
and get her bangle for a keepsake.
She won't make much fuss.

(says _Horace_, _more_ _or_ _less_)

1977

BASIL BUNTING

Uncollected Poems

Edited by
RICHARD CADDEL

Oxford   New York
OXFORD UNIVERSITY PRESS
1991

Oxford University Press, Walton Street, Oxford OX2 6DP

Oxford New York Toronto
Delhi Bombay Calcutta Madras Karachi
Petaling Jaya Singapore Hong Kong Tokyo
Nairobi Dar es Salaam Cape Town
Melbourne Auckland

and associated companies in
Berlin Ibadan

Oxford is a trade mark of Oxford University Press

Uncollected Poems first published in Oxford Poets
as an Oxford University Press paperback 1991

British Library Cataloguing in Publication Data
Data available

Library of Congress Cataloging-in-Publication Data
Bunting, Basil.
[Poems. Selections]
Uncollected poems/Basil Bunting; edited by Richard Caddel.
p. cm. — (Oxford poets)
I. Caddel, Richard, 1949–. II. Title. III. Series.
PR6003.U36A6 1991   821'.914—dc20   91-7937
ISBN 0-19-282870-3

Typeset by Wyvern Typesetting Ltd, Bristol
Printed in Hong Kong

PREFACE

Bunting collected his own poems. The canon which he established in the Fulcrum Press edition of *Collected Poems* (1968) he maintained, with a few corrections and four additional poems in the Oxford University Press edition (1978), up to the year of his death, when he released a single poem for inclusion in the American edition. The present collection does not pretend to alter that.

Instead it draws together those pieces of Bunting's poetry which exist outside that canon: pieces which he at some stage treated as finished, and either published, or intended to publish, or allowed others to publish, or circulated, or simply didn't destroy (he was an expert with fireplace and waste bin). In doing so it performs a slight disservice perhaps to scholars, who enjoy rummaging in obscure places after fugitive items, but this may be offset by the convenience of having the work available. There is sufficient quality in this drawing-together to bring pleasure to scholar, Bunting enthusiast, and general reader alike, and no book needs more justification than that.

Yet critics will say that Bunting would have preferred the work to remain uncollected (the ode which stands as dedicatory inscription to this collection states their case), and to be sure he did not wish to collect the poems, or have them collected, *in his lifetime.* But he cooperated with those who did collect them (notably Roger Guedalla, whose bibliography provides the source in many cases) and sanctioned their recirculation (for instance, in Sister Victoria Forde's thesis, and in the Festschrift for Jonathan Williams): he was fully aware of the interest they would excite, and was never blind to the possibility of a volume such as this. All the work herein is easy to trace in one way or another, if not readily accessible: it is already attracting comment. As critical interest in Bunting grows, some of it has been quoted—not always in context—in critical articles. The need therefore arises to collect this work simply to define it, and distinguish it from work in *Collected Poems.*

In the case of a lesser writer, this would be work of largely surgical interest. However, I confess freely to having enjoyed the task: Bunting's fugitive pieces, though undeniably uneven, are never without quality, and are often of the highest order. 'They Say Etna' and 'Hymn to alias Thor', Pound-pastiche as they are, still read well, and it would be hard to argue the case for continuing to restrict access to work from Bunting's remarkable post-'Briggflatts' period such as 'Such syllables flicker . . .' (Ode 11), or the brief epitaph for Lorine Niedecker (Ode 10).

I have excluded, with some regrets, two surviving pieces of juvenilia, and two limericks. I have also excluded all pieces of dubious ascription (including poems copied by others from notes which Bunting subsequently destroyed), all rough and early versions, and fragments. Against these omissions I am happy to include *The Pious Cat*, Bunting's Northumbrian version of a Persian children's tale. If others can spot glaring oversights in what must be, to some extent, a provisional edition, I hope they will tell me of them. Such other comment as is necessary I have included in the notes at the end of this book, along with citations and sources.

Where variant texts exist I have, with very few exceptions, chosen what appears to be the latest, or most complete version. I have maintained Bunting's orthography, punctuation, and capitalization, with only a few minor exceptions where obvious errors would irritate the reader, or where house style prevailed. In upholding Bunting's preferred textual arrangement (Longer poems/Odes/Overdrafts) I have been faced with difficult decisions (is his Baudelaire too free to be regarded as a translation? should not 'Trinacria' be an overdraft? and so on), where I can only say that I hope my final choices are sufficiently justified by the resulting arrangement. Chronology within each section is never more than approximate. In short, the intention has been to create a readable equivalent to *Collected Poems*: just as so many poets have gained from that volume, so I feel there are few who have nothing to learn from this.

I am fortunate in having had the support and encouragement of Sima Bunting, Tom and Maria Bunting, and John Halliday, of the estate of Basil Bunting, for this project: to them I offer this book, with my thanks. Thanks are due to others too: to Northern Arts, who supplied a writer's award which enabled me to complete part of the work; to my colleagues at Durham University Library; to individuals such as Diana Collecott, Sister Victoria Forde, Harry Gilonis, Roger Guedalla, Peter Makin, Peter Quartermain, Jacqueline Simms, Paul Starkey, Gael Turnbull, Eliot Weinberger, and Jonathan Williams for their comments and advice, and to my family, for their support and patience. Errors and oversights are my own.

Richard Caddel
Durham, July 1990

ACKNOWLEDGEMENTS

Acknowledgement must be made to various libraries and archives for their help and for specific permissions: to the Basil Bunting Poetry Archive, University Library, University of Durham, for permission to reproduce 'Such syllables flicker out of grass', 'Hi, tent-boy, get that tent down', 'You've come! O how flustered and anxious . . .', 'Ginger, who are you going with?', 'That filly couldn't carry a rider', 'Snow's on the fellside, look!', and *The Pious Cat*; to the Collection of American Literature, Beinecke Rare Book and Manuscript Library, Yale University, for permission to reproduce poems from *Caveat Emptor*; to the Harry Ransom Humanities Research Center, University of Texas at Austin, for permission to reproduce 'Envoi to the Reader', 'Amru'l Qais and Labīd and Akhtal', 'Noah's son' and Bunting's comment on that piece; to the Poetry/Rare Books Collection, University Libraries, University at Buffalo, Buffalo, NY, for 'A Song for Rustam' and 'To abate what swells'; and to Oxford University Press for permission to reproduce the Ode 'To a Poet who advised me to preserve my fragments and false starts' (*Collected Poems*, 1978).

The cartoon and photograph of Basil Bunting on the cover are reproduced from the Basil Bunting Poetry Archive by kind permission of the University Library, University of Durham, as is the frontispiece reproduction of the MS version of 'Snow's on the fellside, look!'

CONTENTS

To a Poet who advised me to preserve
my fragments and false starts

Narciss, my numerous cancellations prefer
slow limpness in the damp dustbins amongst the peel
tobacco-ash and ends spittoon lickings litter
of labels dry corks breakages and a great deal

of miscellaneous garbage picked over by
covetous dustmen and Salvation Army sneaks
to one review-rid month's printed ignominy,
the public detection of your decay, that reeks.

Basil Bunting, 1929

THEY SAY ETNA

THEY SAY ETNA

They say Etna
belches as much poison
as Duisburg's pudenda
a littering sow
helpless in the railroad ditch.

        Gear and gear.

The Muses Ergot and Appiol,
                Mr Reader.
Mr Reader,
        the Muses Ergot and Appiol.
What violence or fraud
shall we record?

Popone or Kreuger?
A skipper of the Middle Passage
stinkproof and deaf
with a hundred and seventy slaves
damaged in transit
for Jamaica?

        Gear and gear.

Shall we consider the evidence in Hatry's case?
Or take Lord Bunting—or
           UKASE.
     No one to be found outside his own village
           without
        PAPERS.

   Also, to encourage more efficient tillage,
   2/3 of the produce to be presented to the temporal lord,
   1/5 of the produce to be presented to the parish pope.
       Yours you may say lovingly
              Boris Godunof.
Or Stalin.

*

Item, the Duke of Slumberwear can get more
by letting the shooting although there is nothing to shoot
but a dozen diseased grouse and a few thin leveret
than by cleaning the ditches to make the ground healthy for sheep.

Lord Cummingway, Lord Tommanjerry, gear and gear,
Lord St Thomas and the Duke of Oppenham
think coals too cheap and costs too dear.

* * * * *
* * * * *
*

Gear, then, and gear,
                    gritty-grinding.
The governor spins, raises its arms.
Two three-inch steel cables scream from the drum
seventy fathoms.
We carry lighted Davy lamps,
stoop along narrow track.
Trucks scold tunnel.
In a squat cavern a
naked man on his
knees with a
pickaxe rips a nugget from the coalface.

Four lads
            led the pownies
a mile and a half through rising water,
lampless because the stife
asphyxiates lamps,
by old galleries to the North Shaft.
The water rose.
            The others
came five months later when it was pumped out
and were buried by public subscription.
(The widows were provided for.)
                    *

Sing, Ergot and Appiol, didactically:
'Toil! Accumulate Capital!'
Capital is land upon which
work has been done (*vide* textbooks).
Capital is everything except the desert,
sea, untunnelled rock, upper air.
Breathed air
is Capital, though not rented:
70 million tons of solid matter
suspended in the atmosphere,
November, in London,
not by an act of God.

'The sea is his and he
made it'—Who
made Holland and whose is it?

**MAN IS NOT AN END-PRODUCT,
MAGGOT ASSERTS.**

Make? For the making? The system limps.
Everything in this category is deformed,
even the bookkeeping.
Waste accumulates at compound interest.

**MAN IS AN END-PRODUCT AFFIRMS
BLASPHEMOUS BOLSHEVIK.**

ODES

1

Coryphée gravefooted precise, dance to the gracious music
Thoughts make moving about, dance to the mind's delicate symphony.

2 AGAINST THE TRICKS OF TIME

Why should I discipline myself to verse
Blasting everyday occurrences
With a false flavour of longevity,
Malignantly prolonging
Two corsets in a shop window,
Mumbling indiscreet apologies as now
For what is singularly my own affair,
Or prophesying Death, the kind unmaker
In whom no man has faith? Utterly poet, therefore
Adrift, perusing neglected streets, I
Suppose I ought to be ashamed of myself.

Farewell, ye sequent graces,
Voided faces, still evasive!
Silent be our leave-taking
And mournful

As your night-wanderings
In unlit rooms or where the glow
Of wall-reflected street-lamp-light
The so slow moon

Or hasty matches shadowed large
And crowded out by imps of night
Glimmer on cascades of
Fantom dancers.

Airlapped and silent Muses of light!
Cease to administer
Poisons to dying memories to stir
Pangs of old rapture,

Cease to conspire
Reunions of the inevitable seed
Long blown, barren, sown, gathered
Haphazard to wither.

The dragon rides the middle air like an irresistible wind
Flowing from and to all quarters simultaneously.
His birth is cloudlike of the sea and sun,
Dispersion his life, his death acclaiming voices.
He is the foe, the harbinger. The saints invoke
Michael PROPTER NOS HOMINES ET PROPTER
NOSTRAM SALUTEM but the silent dragon's
Insinuated claw in wincing souls
Answers their supplication. He abets
Indifference with ceaseless splendour
Smudging sketched tables valiantly renewed.
He unsays all words that have passed between men.

3 READING X'S COLLECTED WORKS

I. . .
cemetery of other men's bastards let
wane and peter out
because I am jealous of the Muse's fornications
and over timid to be a cuckold!

Meanwhile you
have raised a sufficient family of versicles;
like you in the main.

STRENGTH
inked with a light brush
in the copper kettledrum.

Strength,
the edges turned down.

(Inverted scorpion)
Focus, strength,
focus of percussions.

Sky convenient in conversation, viz.,
for efficiency's sake,
blindness to the street

where a taxidriver
cocks his patentleather cappeak
perpendicularly over a squint at the weather
calculating chances
of reaching rank's head before lunch.

Or, the neatcreased laundryfresh handkerchief
might anticipate a sneeze
(if linen web trembles to thinking's tuning)

at any nose's tauttipped touch,
receive in convulsion of bloom
snot,

lap over and
cherish till desiccated.

Such charges, coupled lightning,
the rainbow signature on each scroll warrants
genuine, beware of imitations!

The soil refuses the lightning!
Desolate air stagnates over that valley,
winds putrefy, silence, the offered storm

limp, dust hangs damp,
thin mud sags in the air,
a deathstink 's over the whole valley,

vinestakes' curtain of leaves droop
mottled blue with wash,
hard peaches, bitter figs,
the stream niggard trickle of gall,

and flies drag sweat over the eyelids
and sour lips.

Oftener the soil accepts the lightning.

The flat land lies under water
hedge-chequer-grill above concealing
(not long) heliotrope monotony.

Cold water shin-embracing clacks
desolately, no overtones. Lukewarm
moist socks trickle sea-boot squeezed
black gutters muttering between the toes.
Moreover it rains, drizzles.

Utter-horizon-penetrating glances
spoil only paupers towing derelict home
the flat land hedge-grilled heliotrope under water.

Gertie Gitana's hymn to waltzing,
come to think of it, that's the goods.
You, thirdrate muse, Polymnia-alias-Echo,
who'll foster our offspring
begotten in a Waterloo Road three-and-sixpenny
                                          bed-and-breakfast
between indifference and bad habit
established by Erasmus and other idiots
nuts on the classics?
No inclination,
inclination at the wrong time, soul
not at home to callers:
its possibly ultimate inhumation
made flesh under a neat strewing of granite chips
complete with kerb. (But no stone,
Sadi's right, dogs would piss on it.)
Without science, if you please, or psychology!
A mere prescription, as:
'Take one look at the truth about yourself,
you'll never want another.'

'An odds-on favorite's unexciting but
dont back outsiders, its a mugs game',
out of the *selva oscura*, oracle
without authority, 'give over swanking.'

Omar observed: 'Sobriety is unworthy
of anything that has life.' Supplemented
that proposition: 'Turf's pretty till
our grave's turf's pretty.'

Then Barbara
bribing the brain with dud cheques
for any figure on the Bank of Aeolus
(paid up capital twentyone consonants
and five vowels, debtor to
sundry windbags sundry bags of wind,
cent per cent cover in the vaults, vocables
on call or short notice to any amount)
made up so skilfully you wouldnt know her
works the same con-game on the same dupe twice.

Muleteers recite Firdusi, scots sing Burns.
Precedent allows
a moder-rate kettledr-rum r-r-roulade. In practice
keep an eye on the crocodiles, all power
to the congress of murdering crocodiles.
Or check up that syncopated
metre a rising sea never
conforms to?
Double-tongueing a corked flute
descant to the bass:
'Less three per cent deducted for
our compulsory Superannuation Fund.'

O, 'count upon it as a truth next to your creed
that no one person in office of which he is master for life
will ever hazard that office for the good of his country,'
no pedant with established circulation
take Polymnia's hand.
Gertie Gitana's hymn to waltzing
's the goods, you third-rate muse
with your head in the gas oven.

7 ENVOI TO THE READER

From above the moon
    to below the fishes
nobody knows
    my secret heart.
Do you suppose
    I'd publish it?
Spell out a fart
    and have it printed?

1

Child, I have counted
all the stones in this wall...

Even today
to find you alone at home
was impossible.

2

My prospective brother-in-law
sent me a gift, a fan.
It had three different colours,
rose, scarlet and gold.

Everybody asked me:
What did that fan of yours cost you?
I answered: Nothing. My
sister's sweetheart gave it me.

3

On highest summits dawn comes soonest.
(But that is not the time to give over loving.)

4

I went to Hell: never before had I been there!
I did not want to see my sweetheart.

She said to me: Scoundrel and dog!
These pains I undergo on your account.

I said to her: You did not love me,
there are fairer women than you.

Tears are for what can be mended,
not for a voyage ended
the day the schooner put out.
Short fear and sudden quiet
too deep for a diving thief.
Tears are for easy grief.

My soil is shorn,
forests and corn.
Winter will bare the rock.
What has he left of pride
whose son is dead?
My soil has shaved its head.

The sky withers and stinks.
star after star sinks
into the west, by you.
Whirling, spokes of the wheel
hoist up a faded day,
its sky wrinkled and grey.

Words slung to the gale
stammer and fail:
'Unseen is not unknown,
unkissed is not unloved,
unheard is not unsung;'
Words late, lost, dumb.

Truth that shone is dim,
lies cripple every limb.
Where you were, you are not.
Silent, heavy air
stifles the heart's leap.
Truth is asleep.

To abate what swells
use ice for scalpel.
It melts in its wound
and no one can tell
what the surgeon used.
Clear lymph, no scar,
no swathe from a cheek's bloom.

Such syllables flicker out of grass:
'What beckons goes'; and no glide lasts
nor wings are ever in even beat long.
A male season with paeonies, birds bright under thorn.
Light pelts hard now my sun's low,
it carves my stone as hail mud
till day's net drapes the haugh,
glaze crackled by flung drops.
What use? Elegant hope, fever of tune,
new now, next, in the fall, to be dust.

Wind shakes a blotch of sun,
flatter and tattle willow and oak alike
sly as a trout's shadow on gravel.
Light stots from stone, sets ridge and kerf quick
as shot skims rust from steel. Men of the north
'subject to being beheaded and cannot avoid it
of a race that is naturally given that way'.
'Uber sophiae sugens' in hourless dark,
their midnight shimmers like noon.
They clasp that axle fast.

Those who lie with Loki's daughter,
jawbones laid to her stiff cheek,
hear rocks stir above the goaf;
but a land swaddled in light? Listen, make out
lightfall singing on a wall mottled grey
and the wall growls, tossing light,
prow in tide, boulder in a foss.
A man shrivels in many days, eyes thirst for night
to scour and shammy the sky
thick with dust and breath.

Dentdale conversation

Yan tan tethera pethera pimp
nothing to waste but nothing to skimp.
Lambs and gimmers and wethers and ewes
what do you want with political views?
Keep the glass in your windows clear
where nothing whatever's bitter but beer.

13

Now we've no hope of going back,
cutter, to that grey quay
where we moored twice and twice unwillingly
cast off our cables to put out at the slack
when the sea's laugh was choked to a mutter
and the leach lifted hesitantly with a stutter
and sulky clack,

how desolate the swatchways look,
cutter, and the chart's stained,
stiff, old, wrinkled and uncertain,
seeming to contradict the pilot book.
On naked banks a few birds strut
to watch the ebb sluice through a narrowing gut
loud as a brook.

Soon, while that northwest squall wrings out its cloud,
cutter, we'll heave to
free of the sands and let the half moon do
as it pleases, hanging there in the port shrouds
like a riding light. We have no course to set,
only to drift too long, watch too glumly, and wait,
wait.

OVERDRAFTS

Night swallowed the sun as
the fish swallowed Jonas.

(Sa'di)

Many well-known people have been packed away in cemeteries,
there is no longer any evidence that they ever existed.
That old corpse they shovelled under the dirt,
his dust's so devoured not a bone of him's left.

Naushervan's honourable name survives because he was
                                        open-handed,
though a lot has happened since Naushervan died.
— Better be open-handed, What's-your-name, (write it off:
                                        Depreciation)
before the gossip goes: 'What's-his-name's dead.'

(Sa'di)

Light of my eyes, there *is* something to be said.
Drink and give to drink while the bottle is full.
Old men speaking from experience, as I told you:
'Indeed, you will grow old.
Love has respectable people chained up for the torture.
You'd like to rumple his hair? Give up being good.
Rosary and veil have no such relish as drink.'

Put it in practice. Send for the wine-merchant.
Amongst the drinkers, one lifetime,
one purse cannot cramp you.
A hundred lives for your dear!
(In love's business the devil lacks not ideas,
but listen, listen with your heart to the angel's message.)

Maple leaves wither, gaiety's not everlasting.
Wail, O harp! Cry out, O drum!
May *your* glass never want wine!
Look gently behind you and drink.
When you step over the drunks in your gold-scattering gown
spare a kiss for *Hafiz* in his flannel shirt.

(Hafiz)

O everlastingly self-deluded!
    If there's no love for you there's nothing for it
but to go crazy. Anyway, dont set up for
    a paragon of self-restraint.
Love's dizziness cant invade a head
    dizzy with alcohol?
You're jaundiced, misery-hideous!
    Anybody can read your symptoms.
Give respectability and pride the go-by, *Hafiz*,
cadge yourself a drop of booze and get
                        crapulously drunk.

(Hafiz)

Isnt it poetical, a chap's mind in the dumps?
Of course our cliché's true:
'Your lips the seal on my passport
that's a hundred empires in hand.'
So, my heart, dont wince when they mock you,
mockeries rightly regarded are riches:
who doesnt take ghoulish sarcasms thus,
his marble was hacked out in haste.
Wine and tears in a cup—each offers it someone;
that's only polite, under Providence:
the routine of the perfumery business,
one rose crushed, one kept.
And it's false, the frenzy quitting *Hafiz*,
the durable frenzy warranted to

                   last ever so long.

(Hafiz)

I'm the worse for drink again, it's
got the better of me.
A thousand thanks to the red wine
put colour in my face.
I'll kiss the hand that gathered the grapes.
May he never trudge who trod them out!

You'd dock my drink for the fast, you!
God doesn't trifle.
Born with 'Rake' scrawled
on my forehead, dare you erase it?
Talk about wisdom! When it comes to dying
the soul may struggle—like a doomed hero.

Settle down, no nagging, placidity
's silk next your skin. If you
want eternity do so
they'll never use past tense of you.
Drink as *Hafiz*, you'll gather impetus
world without end.

(Hafiz)

From FARIDUN'S SONS

Faridun watched the road
and the army missed the young king.
When the time came for his homecoming
they were getting a welcome ready,
wine, music and dancers.
They had fetched the drums and led the elephants
out of the stable,
hung the whole land with garlands.
. . . A cloud of dust on the road,
presently a fast camel,
a rider in mourning, keening,
a gold box on his lap,
in the box a piece of brocade,
in the brocade. . . !
Came to Faridun,
pale, crying, sighing woe,
they could not make out what he said,
prised the lid off the box,
snatched the cloth, there was Iraj's head.
Faridun fell from his horse like a dead man.
The army tore their clothes,
not for this the king
led them out, this return, torn flags,
drums reversed, drawn faces;
kettledrums, elephants foreheads, draped black,
the horses splashed with indigo,
a dismounted general, an army dismounted,
dust on their heads, officers gnawing their arms,
or calling out:
                    'Never fancy Fate favours you,
the heavens turning above us
ready to snatch whatever they smile on.
Defy them, they smile. Call them Friend,
they never return your devotion.'

To Iraj's garden,
merry at festival time,
Afaridun with unsteady steps,
clutching the young king's head,

his son's head.
He looked at the gorgeous throne—
tawdry without the king,
and the pool, the cypresses,
rosetrees, willows, quinces.
When they strewed dust on the throne
a wail from the army,
groaning, tearing their hair, shedding tears,
clawing their own cheeks.
Faridun put on the ritual crimson sash,
set the pleasure house alight,
dug up the flowerbeds, burned the cypresses,
all the eye's delight,
and hugging Iraj's head turned to heaven:

'God of justice, see how the innocent fare!
His head, the marks of the knife on the neck, I have it.
His body, devoured.
Scald those cruel hearts, let their days be black, all,
blister their hearts, let their hurts fester
till brute beasts pity them.
You who adjust all things, let me find refuge from Time
till I see one of Iraj's blood make ready for vengeance,
till I see those heads cut off like this innocent head.
Then of your mercy let the soil take my measure.'

He mourned so long on the bare ground
his beard grew down to his chest. Wept his sharp eyes blind,
behind closed doors in the great hall.
'You brave young man, no king ever died as you did,
no king beheaded by devils
wild beasts' maws his coffin.'

There was such crying and keening
even the animals could get no sleep.
Assemblies, every man and woman
throughout the country with tears in their eyes,
in black, past consolation,
many a day, as though all life were death.

(Firdosi)

BAUDELAIRE IN CYTHERA

Heart trapezing gaily about the ropes: hull
a-roll under a clear sky.
                              —That sombre beach?
—Songfamous Cythera.
                              —Indeed?
                                        —Yes,
bachelor's paradise. Look at it. . . wretched place!
Festivals of love, eh?. . . whispers and all that?

The moist smell of amours clings to it, isle of blown
roses, still adored. Devout whimpers drift
above like pollen, like ringdove murmurs. A harsh
stony hungry land, harassed by shrill cries.
Nothing Baedeker stars: though I did see something. . .

Not a temple shaded by ancient planes, nor yet
a young priestess of love slacking her tunic to
feel the breeze. We ranged very close in shore,
so close our sails set the birds fluttering over a
black gallows cut out of the sky.

                              They were perched on
carrion, their beaks driven precisely into
putrid sores. The eyes, rotted. Heavy bowels
dangling. Vultures had castrated him. Dogs
were howling.

               Cytherean!
Child of sublime skies! Comic corpse, wretched
contemptible corpse!

Bright sky, shining sea, Venus' land; Baudelaire
bows to Baudelaire through the looking-glass.

(After Baudelaire)

Amru'l Qais and Labīd and Akhtal and blind A'sha and Qais
who keened over the bones of dead encampments and fallen tents,
as we mourn for the ruins of poetry and broken rhymes——
Bu Nuvās and Bu Haddād and Bu Malik bin al Bashar,
Bu Duvaid and Bu Duraid and Ibn Ahmad. Do you hear
him who sang 'She has warned us,' who sang 'The honest sword,'
who sang 'Love has exhausted'——?
Bu'l Ata and Bu'l Abbās and Bu Salaik and Bu'l Mathil,
and the bard of Lavaih and the Harper of Herat.
Where are the wise Afghans, Shuhaid and Rudaki,
and Bu Shakūr of Balkh and Bu'l Fath of Bust likewise.
Bid them come and see our noble century
and read our poetry and despair——

(Manuchehri)

Night is hard by. I am vexed and bothered by sleep.
Dear my girl, bring me something to cure me of sleep.
Not quick and alert, as well be dead as asleep:
what argument have the dead? How shall the sleeping answer?

I for one strive not to die before my time.
Who shall hire the untimely dead? Have they compensation?
I snatch the sleep from my eyes with strong wine,
aye! with strong wine, foe of a young man's sleep.

Much do I wonder at him whom sleep bears away
where there is yet a bottle of wine in the house,
and yet more wonder at him who drinks without music,
without an air on the harp, guzzles his wine.
No horse will drink without you whistle to him:
is a man less than a horse, water more than wine?

Three things, and the more the better, nourish the free:
one is wine and one is music and one is meat.
No cash let there be among us, no book, no dice:
these are three things unfitting to our freedom.
Books to the school, cash to the marketplace,
dice to the taverns of the low.
We, men of wine are we, meat are we, music. . .
Well, then! wine have we, meat have we, music. . .

(Manuchehri)

You, with my enemy, strolling down my street,
you're a nice one! Aren't you ashamed to meet me?
Didn't you call me 'malignant', and 'quarrelsome'?
Don't you complain of my 'impossible' character?

You looked round and found someone more to your liking.
You escaped neatly from my 'temper' and 'dullness'.
Plainly, your love is flooding his brook:
the day is gone when it trickled into mine.

Now that you've found someone such as you wanted
why do you blunder so far down my street?

(Manuchehri)

The thundercloud fills meadows with heavenly beauty,
gardens with plants, embroiders plants with petals,
distils from its own white pearls brilliant dyes,
makes a Tibet of hills where its shadow falls,
San'a of our fields when it passes on to the desert.
Wail of the morning nightingale, scent of the breeze,
frenzy a man's bewildered, drunken heart.
Now is the season lovers shall pant awhile,
now is the day sets hermits athirst for wine.

Shall I sulk because my love has a double heart?
Happy is he whose she is singlehearted!
She has found me a new torment for every instant
and I am, whatever she does, content, content.
If she has bleached my cheek with her love, say: Bleach!
Is not pale saffron prized above poppy red?
If she has stooped my shoulders, say to them: Stoop!
Must not a harp be bent when they string it to sing?
If she has kindled fire in my heart, say: Kindle!
Only the kindled candle sends forth light.
If tears rain from my eyes, say: Let them rain!
Spring rains make fair gardens. And if then
she has cast me into the shadow of exile, say:
Those who seek fortune afar find it the first.

(Manuchehri)

Hi, tent-boy, get that tent down.
The first are gone and one drum's growled,
loads on the camels, nearly prayer-time,
and tonight full moon, up as soon
as the sun drops behind Babyl.

O silver-white Sanubar! Could a day
fade without our noticing?
Leave me now, lovely girl.
There'll be no harvest of the love we sowed.

—Tears pelting as though pepper thrown
had blistered her eyes, stumbling and fluttering
she belted her arms around me,
hung as a sword hangs, crying:
'Is it to please all jealous Primnesses?
How can I tell whether you will come back?
Perfect I thought you in every art,
but in love you are not perfect.'
And I: 'I am no tyro.
Love's taste's sharpest at a hasty parting.'

Patience heavy on my heart, I looked
where the tents had been, and the camels,
saw neither mount nor rider
but my Najib, restless;
loosed the hobbles from her knees
like one releasing a bird from a fowler's net;
made the headstall fast at her ears' root,
slung the blanket loose to her shoulder,
mounted. She leapt to go,
I praying: 'God make it easy',
counting her steps for the stages
as surveyors measure the ground,
into a hard, cold desert.
Wind froze my blood, the pools frozen
like silver dishes on a gold tray.

Before morning night was blacker
for the white snow wasting away
and out of the hard ground rose a mud like fishglue.
One long watch of the night
was done when the Dogstar rose
bright over Mosul's mound,
then the Great Bear, and I came close
behind the caravan like a boat nearing the beach.
The sound of their anklets reached me
with chatter and clatter of bells
and I saw the peacock litters
stilted on herony legs;
bells within bells, gilded,
hanging to the camels' knees,
and lances, making the valley a cornfield.

(After Manuchehri)

You've come! O how flustered and anxious I've been,
chill as a stone ever since you went away
but not forgetful; silent, yes, and confused,
longing, longing always to see you again.

Without you I've not slept, not once, in the garden
nor cared much whether I slept on holly or flock,
lonely to death between one breath and the next
only to meet you, hear you, only to touch;

waiting all night for the breeze to bring me your scent
till the cocks called up the sun from jail, and
poppy, peony, primula glowed yet I
shivered and sank, sick for consolation
sick day long for the pain of your going, saying
'You broke your word. I have stood fast by mine.'

You broke your word. I have stood fast by mine,
counting old kisses, tasting past praise again,
a heavy, cumbersome bundle not to set down;
but 'Keep' you said. I've let no dust of it drop.

Thorns in our tangled garden pock my cheeks
when I go down to the burn, eyes turned in
from day to a night in my head, your night,
heavy for ever over the garden now.

At the heel of my door they'll ask what fruit life bore.
Tell them the night I talked with my darling was sweet.
Who has judged that the bond you gave then is null,
judged unjustly. I have performed my part.
Will you be glad one day to hear me greet you:
'You've come. O how flustered and anxious I've been.'

(After Sa'di)

Ginger, who are you going with?
Some slim kid? One who squeezes you
among the early meadowsweet?
You do your hair to please him,
or he thinks so, loose and smooth.

Change your mind and he'll cry.
He's not reckoned with storms
but fancies your glow is
all for him, always at hand,
always gentle; winds don't veer.

You'll shine on them all, poor brats,
till one of them gets you.
But as for me,
I've wrung my shirt out long since.

(Horace)

43

Like a fawn you dodge me, Molly,
a lost fawn.
A breath of wind scares her.
Leaves rustle, or a rabbit
stirs, and her heart flutters,
her knees quiver.
But it's me chasing you, Molly,
not a tiger, not to tear you.
Let mother go,
you're old enough for a man.

(Horace)

That filly couldnt carry a rider nor
pull her weight in a plow team. How
could she stand up under a stallion?
All she thinks about is fields or a
brook when it's warm to plodge in.
Prancing round with the colts is her fun. Why
bite green apples? Come October they'll redden.
Then she'll match you: Time will give her the years
it snatches from you. She'll toss her head soon
to challenge a man, the besom, cuter
than Jane who hides or Leslie who lets her blouse
slip from her shining shoulder or even Jimmy.
You cant tell him from a girl if he keeps his mouth shut
with his long, loose hair and unguessable face.

(Horace)

Snow's on the fellside, look! How deep;
our wood's staggering under its weight.
The burns will be tonguetied
while frost lasts.

But we'll thaw out. Logs, logs for the hearth!
and dont spare my good whisky. No water, please.
Forget the weather. Elm and ash
will stop signalling
when this gale drops.

Why reckon? Why forecast? Pocket
whatever today brings,
and dont turn up your nose, it's childish,
at making love and dancing.
When you've my bare scalp, if you must, be glum.

Keep your date in the park while light's whispering.
Hunt her out, well wrapped up, hiding and giggling,
and get her bangle for a keepsake.
She wont make much fuss.

(Says Horace, more or less)

Poor soul! Softy, whisperer,
hanger-on, pesterer, sponge!
Where are you off to now?
Pale and stiff and bare-bummed,
It's not much fun in the end.

(Hadrian)

THE PIOUS CAT

THE PIOUS CAT

by Obaid-e Zakani (and Basil Bunting)

By your leave!

Sagacious and circumspect persons, attend!
This is a story of cats and mice,
how constantly they quarrel and contend.
It is short, truthful and precise.
Listen sharply. Do not miss a minute,
there is so much meaning and deep wisdom in it,
and learned science and politic guile
and rime and rhetoric and style.

By Heaven's decree there was a cat
in Haltwhistle, rough, rich and fat.
His fur was like a coat of mail
with lion's claws and leopard's tail.
When he went out and wailed at night
he made policemen shake with fright.
When he crouched in a flowerbed
big game hunters turned pale with dread.
All creatures beside him seemed tame.
Tibbald was this hero's name.

One day he visited the cellar
to scout for mice. Behind a pillar
he lay in ambush like a bandit
and it fell out as he had planned it—
a mouse crept from a crack and squeaked,
then leapt on a cask of beer (that leaked)
to drink, and shortly drank again.
Beer made him truculent and vain.
He snapped his fingers. 'Where's the cat?
I'll make his skin into a doormat.
I'll teach him: I'll give him what-for.
Cats? One good mouse can lick a score!
Tibbald! Who's he? Let him sneer and purr,
he'll cringe to me. The cat's a cur!'

51

Tibbald kept mum, but in the pause
you could hear him sharpening his teeth and claws
When they were keen he made one jump
and caught the drunken mouse by the rump.

Mouse said: 'Please mister, let me off!
I did not mean to boast and scoff.
What I said was said in liquor,
and tipsy tongues talk ten times quicker
than sober sense. Dont bear a grudge!'
but Tibbald only answered: 'Fudge!
Bring your remarks to a fullstop,'
then ate him and lapped the gravy up.

Next Tibbald went to the wash basin
he used to scrub his hands and face in,
and brushed his tail and combed his hair
and went to church and said this prayer:

'Lord, I confess the awful vice
of breakfasting on little mice;
but, Father, I repent sincerely.
I will pay—not a pittance merely
but more than ample compensation.
To every surviving relation
or legal representative
of my poor victim, I will give. . .
some cold coffee and plenty of tea
(on proper proof of identity,
birth certificate and passport
and other documents of that sort);
and I will gobble no more mice
in stews or sausages or pies
nor *table d'hôte* nor *à la carte*.
An humble and a contrite heart
thinks lettuces and things like that
as sweet as a tender farmyard rat.'
Here his repentance went so deep
that Tibbald could not choose but weep.

A mouse had hidden behind the pulpit.
He heard Tib's sob and watched him gulp it,
then ran all the way home and blurted:
'Good news! the cat has been converted!
He has turned charitable and meek
and means to fast six days a week,
and on the seventh he will eat
acorns and trash instead of mouse-meat.'
So all the mice cried: 'Halleluia!
You dont suppose he'll relapse though, do ye?'

To give their gratitude a vent
seven eminent mice were sent
to take Saint Tibbald a testimonial.
They marched with dignified ceremonial
and every mouse of them had brought
gifts of the most expensive sort.
The first mouse brought a bottle of Schiedam.
The second brought a roast leg of lamb.
The third mouse brought a red currant tart;
the fourth, spaghetti by the yard;
the fifth, hot dogs with Cocacola.
The sixth brought bread and gorgonzola.
The seventh mouse brought a homemade
plumcake and a jug of lemonade.
Their manners were courteous and wellbred.
They bowed respectfully and said:
'Long live the cat! May we enquire,
is your health all you can desire?
Deign to accept this trifling token
of compliments we will leave unspoken.'

'Upon my word' said Tib, 'here's dinner!
Since breakfast, I have got much thinner
by fasting. Service and self denial
were evidently worth the trial
since Just and Merciful Providence
sends me the Reward of Abstinence.
It sees my worth (Who can deny it?)
and furnishes me a richer diet.

I am sure a good conscience always led
to a larger share of Daily Bread.
Dear friends! Kind comrades! Fellow creatures!
Come nearer. Let me see your features.'

The mice were flustered and in a dither
but they stepped forward all together
until they came within arm's length.
Then Tibbald suddenly showed his strength
and skill, and in a little moment
they found out what fair words from a foe meant,
for two to left and two to right
and one between his jaws to bite
(that makes five) he caught in so cunning a way
that only two were saved by running away.

'Woe and disaster! Fellow mice,
can you stand by and watch your neighbours
guzzled before your very eyes?
Quick, oil your rifles, whet your sabres.
This foul aggression must be fought out.'
Then all the mice cried: 'Shame and pity!
Refer the facts to a committee
and while they are getting a report out
we'll have our mourning made to order,
hem handkerchiefs with a black border
to wipe our turbulent tears away
with due and dignified delay
until they tell us the King of Mice is
ready to meet this urgent crisis.'

The king was grave and proud and prim.
They brought him the report to skim.
The gist and pith of it was that:
'Oh King, consider the cruel cat.
Once on a time that ravenous ratter ate
his daily mouse at a steady flat rate
but since he took to prayers and pieties
he bolts us down by whole societies.'

54

On this, His Majesty undertook
to bring the criminal cat to book
and signed a royal proclamation
to mobilise the entire nation
with rifles, bayonets, pistols, shells,
swords, gasmasks and whatever else
might come in handy on a campaign,
such as antidotes against rat-bane.

His general held a grand parade
where twenty regiments displayed
smart uniforms of every shade.
Their caps were stiff, their buttons bright,
belts and boots polished, blouses tight,
hair cut, trousers pressed, webbing white,
and ribbons blazed on every bust.
The swaggering general staff discussed:
'What are our war aims? How shall we state 'em?
What must we put in our ultimatum?
Breach of treaty? Gross atrocity?'
but when they had whittled away their verbosity
the king's ambassador, grave and sly,
carried this message: 'Submit or die.'

Now stop your ears, maid, matron, bride!
Switch off your hearing aids and hide
your faces in your wraps and shawls,
for Tibbald answered roughly: '⁜'.
But when he had watched the messenger mount, he
called all the cats he could find in the county
and drilled them daily on the fells
to scratch, bite, and fire off rockets and shells
till one cold dawn they saw the host
of mice advancing from the coast.

Grim was the onslaught! Dead and dying
lay close as chipped potatoes frying,
with hiss, roar, groan and bubble.
Arms, legs, tails, whiskers strewed the moor
like muck spread thick on winter stubble.

⁜ a word in cattish language meaning 'Oh dear me, *what* nonsense!'

A million dead? No, no! Far more.
When Tibbald charged with his best equipped
storm troops, near mouse H.Q. he slipped
and wallowed in the mud. In a trice
he was tied up by nearly a hundred mice.
'Victory' the victors cried.
'Now this war criminal must be tried.'

The warrant was drawn under the king's signet. He
called on the judges for speed and dignity,
so as they assembled to try the crime
they slapped on their black caps to save time,
then sentenced him with solemn squeals
to be hung by the neck and then by the heels.
Fast workmen got the gallows built
while the Bench established Tibbald's guilt.

But while the High Tribunal tried him
the cat was gnawing the thongs that tied him
till with a resolute wrench he bust his
bonds and swallowed the Lord Chief Justice.
King, heroes, hangman, all the hamper,
I wish you could have seen them scamper.

That's where this story comes to a stop.
Now, if you think I made it up
you're wrong. I never. It wasnt me,
it was Obaid-e Zakani.

Note

You must call him 'Obeyed', like the English word 'obeyed a command', 'obeyed a zaw-kaw-nee'; and save most of your breath for the 'nee'. He wrote this story about six hundred years ago, and Persian children still read it at school, or they used to, twenty years since. Any story that lasts as long as that is worth listening to, I think. Perhaps not everything in it is true, but bits of it are very true indeed.

B. Bunting, 1937–77

NOTES

NOTES

With the exception of a single quatrain whose 'circulation' seems to have been largely oral, I have restricted these notes to the purely bibliographical, adding only such comment as seems necessary to establish context. Some archival sources of texts or variants are given. References to Roger Guedalla, *Basil Bunting: a bibliography of works and criticism* (Norwood, PA, 1973) are given as (Guedalla), with the appropriate item reference. The following conventions for Bunting's collections have been used:

(1930): *Redimiculum Matellarum*, Milan, 1930 (Guedalla A1)

(1935): *Caveat Emptor: poems by Basil Bunting*, unpublished TS dated 1935 in the Beinecke Rare Book and Manuscript Library, Yale

(1950): *Poems 1950*, Galveston, 1950 (Guedalla A2)

(1965): *Loquitur*, London, 1965 (Guedalla A5)

(1968): *Collected Poems*, London, 1968 (Guedalla A9)

(1985): *Collected Poems*, Mt Kisco, 1985

THEY SAY ETNA: First published in *Active Anthology*, ed. Ezra Pound, London, 1933 (Guedalla B4). Variant included in (1935). Corrupt variant in (1950); quoted in *Confucius to Cummings: an Anthology of Poetry*, ed. Ezra Pound and Marcella Spann, New York, 1964 (Guedalla B10). Faced with three versions, I have chosen that which seems the most self-contained and complete: in this case, the earliest.

ODES

1: Published as an epigraph in (1930).

2: Published in (1930), included (untitled) in (1935). A version of the central section became 'Farewell ye sequent graces' (Ode 2) from (1950) onwards.

3: Published in *Whips and Scorpions: Specimens of Modern Satiric Verse*, ed. Sherard Vines, Glasgow, 1932 (Guedalla B2). Included with variant title in (1935).

4: Included in (1935).

5: Included in (1935).

6: Included in (1935).

7: TS in the Harry Ransom Humanities Research Center, Austin, Texas: part of a group of poems (including sections of Ode 6, above, and Overdrafts, (Isnt it poetical . . .) sent to Louis Zukofsky in 1935. Appended to title in TS: '(It dont apply to you, Louis)'. Other copies exist, e.g. variant in letter to Ezra Pound (summer 1935) in the Beinecke Rare Book and Manuscript Library.

8: Included in (1935), with an author's note: 'Only 2 & 4 are Sicilian: the other two are from North Italy'. Part 3 became Ode 27 from (1965) onwards.

9: TS in the Poetry/Rare Books Collection, SUNY at Buffalo, dated 1952–1964 (the first date added in ink, possibly in another hand). Also TS in the Harry Ransom Humanities Research Center, Austin, Texas. Included in *Basil Bunting:*

a major British Modernist (Ph.D. thesis, University of Wisconsin) by Barbara E. Lesch, Wisconsin, 1979. Published, with some variant spacing, and dated 7: IX: 64, in *Sulfur* No. 14, ed. Clayton Eshleman, Los Angeles, 1985. Rustam, Bunting's first son, died in 1952.

10: TS in the Poetry/Rare Books Collection, SUNY at Buffalo, dated 1971. Published in *Epitaphs for Lorine*, ed. Jonathan Williams, Champaign, 1973. Lorine Niedecker died in 1970.

11: Some copies typeset by Bunting and circulated to friends *c*.1972 (e.g. in Mountjoy Collection, Basil Bunting Poetry Archive, Durham University Library). Reprinted in *Music and meaning in the poetry of Basil Bunting* (Ph.D. thesis, University of Notre Dame, Ind.) by Sister Victoria Forde, Notre Dame, 1972. A quotation mark in line 16 has been supplied from MS material in the Mountjoy Collection.

12: Dated 1978. Published in *Truck* vol. 21, ed. David Wilk, (Carrboro), 1979.

13: Published in (1985) where it is dated 1980; earlier version dated 1977 published in *Agenda* vol. 16 (i), ed. William Cookson, London, 1978. Released by Bunting for inclusion in (1985) nine days before his death, this poem properly belongs in a definitive British edition of *Collected Poems*.

OVERDRAFTS

I have used Bunting's preferred term for his translations, of which he noted: 'It would be gratuitous to assume that a mistranslation is unintentional.'

'Night swallowed the sun . . .': Published in *A Test of Poetry*, ed. Louis Zukofsky, NY, 1948 (Guedalla B6). Version of Sa'di's *Gulistan*, I, iv. Dated by Zukofsky as '*c*.1935'. The couplet appears as part of a TS entitled 'The Rosegarden, part one: The Habits of Kings. Tale number four' in the Harry Ransom Humanities Research Center, Austin, Texas. This piece is punctuated by verse fragments, including the following:

> Noah's son took to low company:
>   him prophecy ceased to illumine.
> The dog of the Seven Sleepers became,
>   by prolonged good company, human.

'I am very fond of Noah's son and always recite it whenever there's an opportunity' he added. He would still recite it on occasions towards the end of his life.

'Many well-known people . . .': Included in (1935). Version of Sa'di's *Gulistan*, I, ii.

'Light of my eyes . . .': Published in *Bozart-Westminster*, vol. 1 (i), ed. T. Jacobs and E. Hartsock, Oglethorpe, 1935 (Guedalla D10). Included with variants in (1935). Version of Hafiz (see e.g. H. S. Jarrett's edn, Calcutta, 1881, No. 444).

'O everlastingly self-deluded!': Included in (1935). Version of Hafiz (see e.g. Jarrett, No. 503).

'Isnt it poetical . . .': Included in (1935), also variant TS in the Harry Ransom Humanities Research Center, Austin, Texas (see n. on Ode 7 above). Version of Hafiz (see e.g. Jarrett, No. 226).

'I'm the worse for drink. . .': Included in (1935), also variant TS in the Harry Ransom Humanities Research Center, Austin, Texas. Version of Hafiz (see e.g. Jarrett, No. 255).

From *Faridun's Sons*: Published in *The Criterion*, vol. 15, ed. T. S. Eliot, London, 1936 (Guedalla D11). A rough version exists as section 7 of a TS headed (in ink) 'About ⅓ of the story of Faridun's Sons' in the Harry Ransom Humanities Research Center, Austin, Texas, together with other related Firdosi material in draft form. Version of Firdosi's *Shahnameh*, 'Faridun', ll. 543–92 (see e.g. Tehran, 1934).

Baudelaire in Cythera: Included in (1935). Version based on Baudelaire, *Un Voyage à Cythère*.

'Amru'l Qais and Labīd and Akhtal. . .': Fragment from a MS letter to Zukofsky dated May Day 1939. Included in *Music and meaning in the poetry of Basil Bunting*, (Ph.D. thesis, University of Notre Dame, Ind.) by Sister Victoria Forde, Notre Dame, 1972; reprinted in *Basil Bunting: Man and Poet*, ed. Carroll F. Terrell, Orono, 1981. Version of Manuchehri (see e.g. A. Kazimirski's edn, Paris, 1886, No. 87, ll. 9–21).

'Night is hard by . . .': Published in *Nine*, No. 4 (vol. 2 (iii)), ed. Peter Russell, London, 1950 (Guedalla D14). Version of Manuchehri (see e.g. Kazimirski, No. 6).

'You, with my enemy . . .': Published (in an earlier form) in *Nine*, No. 11 (vol. 4 (ii)), ed. Peter Russell, London, 1956 (Guedalla D18). Published thus in *Agenda*, vol. 16, (i), ed. William Cookson, London, 1978, where it is dated 1949. Also MS, with slight variations, in the Basil Bunting Poetry Archive, Durham University Library (Mountjoy Collection) dated 1949. Version of Manuchehri (see e.g. Kazimirski, No. 91).

'The thundercloud fills meadows. . .': Published in *Nine*, No. 11 (vol. 4 (ii)), ed. Peter Russell, London, 1956 (Guedalla D18). The second section, dated 1949, appears on its own from (1965) onwards. Version of Manuchehri (see e.g. Kazimirski, No. 14, ll. 1–12).

'Hi, tent-boy . . .': TS with MS alterations, dated 1949, in Basil Bunting Poetry Archive, Durham University Library (Mountjoy Collection). Version of Manuchehri (see e.g. Kazimirski, No. 29, ll. 1–46).

'You've come!. . .': TS with MS alterations, dated 1974, in Basil Bunting Poetry Archive, Durham University Library (Mountjoy Collection).

'Ginger, who are you going with?': TS with MS alterations, dated 1969, in Basil Bunting Poetry Archive, Durham University Library (Mountjoy Collection). Version of Horace, Odes, I v.

'Like a fawn you dodge me, Molly': TS with MS alteration, undated, in Basil Bunting Poetry Archive, Durham University Library (Mountjoy Collection). Version of Horace, Odes, I xxiii.

'That filly couldnt carry a rider . . .': TS, undated, in Basil Bunting Poetry Archive, Durham University Library (Mountjoy Collection). Version of Horace, Odes, II v.

'Snow's on the fellside, look!. . .': MS in Basil Bunting Poetry Archive, Durham University Library, dated 1977. Published (with variant punctuation) in *Agenda*, vol. 16 (i), ed. William Cookson, London, 1978. Version of Horace, Odes, I ix.

'Poor soul! . . .': Quoted in 'Six Plaints and a Lament for Basil Bunting' by Peter Quartermain, published in *Conjunctions*, vol. 8, ed. Bradford Morrow, NY, 1985. Intended as an ending for an uncompleted longer poem, of which Ode 13 was at one stage an opening (I am grateful to Peter Quartermain for this information). Version of Hadrian (see e.g. Loeb Classical Library, vol. 284: Minor Latin Poets, 1934).

THE PIOUS CAT

Bunting intended this fable to be published as an illustrated book for children. The poem was published in a limited edition by Bertram Rota, in 1986. That edition includes two versions: one from a TS of Bunting's, and one from his MS. This edition follows the MS version. A slightly variant MS is held in the Mountjoy Collection, of the Basil Bunting Poetry Archive, Durham University Library.

OXFORD POETS

Fleur Adcock

Edward Kamau Brathwaite

Joseph Brodsky

Basil Bunting

W. H. Davies

Michael Donaghy

Keith Douglas

D. J. Enright

Roy Fisher

David Gascoyne

Ivor Gurney

David Harsent

Anthony Hecht

Zbigniew Herbert

Thomas Kinsella

Brad Leithauser

Derek Mahon

Medbh McGuckian

Jamie McKendrick

James Merrill

Peter Porter

Craig Raine

Henry Reed

Christopher Reid

Stephen Romer

Carole Satyamurti

Peter Scupham

Penelope Shuttle

Louis Simpson

Anne Stevenson

George Szirtes

Grete Tartler

Edward Thomas

Charles Tomlinson

Chris Wallace-Crabbe

Hugo Williams